Pet Store Subtraction

By Simone T. Ribke

Subject Consultant
Chalice Bennett
Elementary Specialist
Martin Luther King Jr. Laboratory School
Evanston, Illinois

Reading Consultant
Cecilia Minden-Cupp, PhD
Former Director, Language and Literacy Program
Harvard Graduate School of Education

Children's Press®
A Division of Scholastic Inc.
New York   Toronto   London   Auckland   Sydney
Mexico City   New Delhi   Hong Kong
Danbury, Connecticut

Designer: Herman Adler Design
Photo Researcher: Caroline Anderson
The photo on the cover shows a boy and his dog at a pet store.

Library of Congress Cataloging-in-Publication Data

Ribke, Simone T.
  Pet store subtraction / by Simone T. Ribke.
    p. cm. — (Rookie read-about math)
  Includes index.
  ISBN-10: 0-516-29673-6 (lib. bdg.)   0-516-28902-0 (pbk.)
  ISBN-13: 978-0-516-29673-9 (lib. bdg.)   978-0-516-28902-1 (pbk.)
  1. Subtraction—Juvenile literature. I. Title. II. Series.

  QA115.R53 2006
  513.2'12—dc22   2005032747

CHILDREN'S PRESS, and ROOKIE READ-ABOUT®,
and associated logos are trademarks and/or registered trademarks
of Scholastic Library Publishing. SCHOLASTIC and associated logos
are trademarks and/or registered trademarks of Scholastic Inc.

1 2 3 4 5 6 7 8 9 10 R 16 15 14 13 12 11 10 09 08 07

Jen works at a pet store. She needs to figure out how many pets and supplies were sold during the day. Jen will use subtraction to see how many new pets and supplies she needs to order.

This morning, there were four baby ferrets. Jen sold three baby ferrets. She subtracts three ferrets from four ferrets. She writes this number sentence:

$$4 - 3 = 1$$

Four minus three equals one. There is only one baby ferret left. Jen wants to have four ferrets in her pet store.

How many ferrets does Jen
need to order?

This morning, there were twenty parakeets. This afternoon, Jen sold eight parakeets.

How many parakeets are left?

Jen subtracts eight parakeets from twenty parakeets. She writes this number sentence on her chart:

$$20 - 8 = 12$$

There are twelve parakeets left. Jen doesn't need to order parakeets today. She only has to order more when there are fewer than ten left in the store.

This morning, there were seven gerbils. Jen sold two gerbils.

How many gerbils are left?

Jen orders more gerbils if there are fewer than four left.

Jen subtracts two gerbils from seven gerbils. She writes this number sentence on her chart:

$$7 - 2 = 5$$

There are five gerbils left.

Does Jen need to order more gerbils?

13

This morning, there were nine squeaky dog toys in the store. Jen sold four squeaky dog toys. How many dog toys are left?

Jen subtracts four toys from nine toys. She writes this number sentence on her chart:

$$9 - 4 = 5$$

There are five squeaky dog toys left. How many squeaky toys do you think Jen should order? She doesn't want to run out of them!

17

Hermit crabs live in shells. There were twelve hermit crabs when the store opened today. Jen sold six of them. How many are left?

Jen subtracts six hermit crabs from twelve hermit crabs.

$$12 - 6 = 6$$

There are six hermit crabs left. How many hermit crabs does Jen need to order?

The dog collars hang in two rows of ten. There were twenty collars when the store opened. If Jen sold two, how many are left?

Jen subtracts two collars from twenty collars.

$$20 - 2 = 18$$

There are eighteen collars left. Jen only needs to order more collars when there are fewer than ten left. She won't order any collars today.

Jen helped people pick out pets and supplies today.

Subtraction helped Jen figure out what to order. More pets and supplies will be delivered tomorrow.

Pet store subtraction is a lot of fun.

29

Words You Know

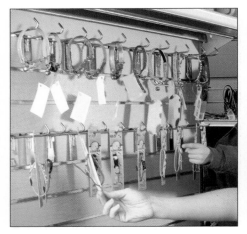

collars

hermit crabs

ferret

gerbils

parakeets

toys

Index

About the Author

Simone T. Ribke is a writer and editor of children's books. Since earning a B.S. in Elementary Education, she has written a wide array of children's books and professional educational materials, including work on a national math education program.

Photo Credits